Essential Issues

DRUG
TRAFFICKING

DRUG
TRAFFICKING

BY JILL SHERMAN

Content Consultant
Sanho Tree
Fellow, Drug Policy Project
Institute for Policy Studies

ABDO
Publishing Company

CREDITS

Published by ABDO Publishing Company, 8000 West 78th Street,
Edina, Minnesota 55439. Copyright © 2010 by Abdo Consulting
Group, Inc. International copyrights reserved in all countries. No
part of this book may be reproduced in any form without written
permission from the publisher. The Essential Library™ is a
trademark and logo of ABDO Publishing Company.

Printed in the United States of America,
North Mankato, Minnesota
102009
012010

 PRINTED ON RECYCLED PAPER

Editor: Melissa Johnson
Copy Editor: Rebecca Rowell
Interior Design and Production: Becky Daum
Cover Design: Becky Daum

Library of Congress Cataloging-in-Publication Data
Sherman, Jill.
  Drug trafficking / Jill Sherman.
     p. cm. — (Essential issues)
  Includes bibliographical references and index.
  ISBN 978-1-60453-953-0
  1. Drug traffic—Juvenile literature. 2. Drug abuse and crime—
Juvenile literature. 3. Drug control—Juvenile literature. I. Title.
  HV5809.5.S44 2010
  363.45—dc22

                                        2009029935

TABLE OF CONTENTS

A Drug Enforcement Administration (DEA) officer removing marijuana plants from a national forest in Washington in 2005

THE DRUG TRADE

From the farmers to the producers, the smugglers, the street dealers, and the users, the drug trade is deeply rooted in the global economy. It is protected and overseen by powerful groups known as drug cartels that make huge profits

from this multibillion-dollar
industry.

Many organizations combat this
illegal business, including local police
and federal agencies. Federal groups
include the Central Intelligence
Agency (CIA), the Federal Bureau
of Investigation (FBI), and the Drug
Enforcement Administration (DEA).
These agencies work in cooperation
with the governments of other
countries and the United Nations.
Numerous other organizations are
also dedicated to controlling the drug
trade and preventing drug use.

What Is Drug Trafficking?

Drug trafficking is another
term for the drug trade. It refers to
the illegal process through which
narcotics and other illegal drugs are
produced, transported, and sold.
Many people are involved at the
various stages of drug trafficking.
It has spread over virtually every part

What Are Drugs?

Drugs are chemical sub-
stances that can be used
to make the body func-
tion differently. Medicinal
drugs can treat or cure a
disease. Antibiotics, for
example, help the body
fight infections.

Illegal drugs are most
often used for recreational,
or nonmedical, purposes.
Cocaine, marijuana, and
methamphetamines are
the most commonly used
illegal drugs in the United
States. These drugs are
used for their mind-
altering or mood-altering
abilities.

of the globe. Most drugs are grown in developing nations. The drugs are then transported to industrialized nations, such as the United States and European countries, where drug use is widespread.

Because drugs are illegal in many parts of the world, drug trafficking is done secretly on the black market. In many places, it is against the law to sell, consume, or simply possess drugs. Depending on the type and quantity of drug found, a person can face lengthy jail time for having drugs. Despite the risks involved in

The Supply Chain

It takes many people to make and bring a product to the customer. The supply chain is the system of how a raw material, such as the coca plant, is processed into cocaine, transported, and sold.

A supply chain starts with the suppliers. Suppliers harvest the raw materials, which come from nature. In the case of drugs, raw materials are crops. When crops are grown and harvested, the growers can sell them.

Once sold, the crops are controlled by drug trade organizations, which prepare, transport, and sell them. They may be responsible for making the drug ready for consumption. Or they may sell the crop in its unprocessed form. The drugs are concealed and transported along predetermined trade routes. As law enforcement actions disrupt trade routes, traders find new routes.

Someone from the cartel usually receives the drugs in the United States or other nations. This person sells the drugs to middlemen, local dealers, or street gangs, which then sell the drugs to users. Drug users are often willing to pay large sums of money for drugs. This keeps the drug trade well funded and makes drug trafficking a profitable business.

drug trafficking, it remains a large industry that continues to spread throughout the world.

The Issue

Drug trafficking is a global problem. In the areas where drug trafficking organizations and cartels operate, violence between rival groups is common. In some cases, the drug trafficking organizations are more powerful, better funded, and more heavily armed than the governments of the countries where they operate.

Drug-related violence is a problem in the United States. Organizations that traffic drugs in the United States compete with one another for turf, or territory, because each group sells drugs in its own specific area. Sometimes, violence breaks out between the members of these organizations or with the police.

Size of the Industry

Bill Alden, a retired DEA agent, first realized how big the cocaine industry was in Colombia after a large drug bust in 1984. Alden recalled, "There was no impact. Almost twelve tons of cocaine was seized, and that had absolutely no impact on the market at all, on availability. It continued just as it did, as ferocious as it was before. And then we really began to realize how big it really was."[1]

The drug trade may also encourage police corruption. Police officers and border guards may accept bribes from drug trafficking organizations in exchange for ignoring their illegal activities. In some cases, law enforcement personnel may actually use their positions to aid criminal activities.

Drug abusers can also pose a burden to society. Along with drug use may come other health risks from sharing dirty needles or accidental overdoses. Hospitals must use resources to care for people who have put themselves in danger. Drug users who become addicts often require additional care. Some recover, but others may never overcome their addiction.

Drug trafficking and drug use cause problems in many areas of society. Virtually no area of the world is left untouched by the drug trade. But controlling the drug trade is often a difficult task.

Drug Enforcement

Drug enforcement agencies do what they can to prevent the

Other Illegal Activity

Firearms trafficking is closely linked to the drug trade. Cartels use firearms from the United States to enforce business deals and defend territory. This activity increases violence at the U.S.-Mexico border. Smugglers also use the routes from the drug trade to transport illegal immigrants across the U.S.-Mexico border.

Drug use and addiction can lead to crime and homelessness. Rehabilitation programs help drug addicts.

continued spread of drug trafficking. Some law enforcement agents destroy crops of marijuana, coca, and other crops used for drugs. Some DEA agents go undercover and enter drug cartels. They acquire information about cartels' activities that leads to arrests. Occasionally, these agencies are able to make a major arrest and seize a large amount of illegal drugs.

An undercover DEA agent (right) spoke with a suspected drug dealer in May 2008.

One such operation came to light in September 2008. Project Reckoning involved a long investigation into one of Mexico's prominent drug organizations: the Gulf Cartel. Project Reckoning featured cooperation among drug enforcement agencies from the United States, Mexico, and Italy. Over the course of two years, these agencies uncovered information about the organization and leaders of the Gulf Cartel.

Finally, on September 17, 2008, agents were ready to make arrests. Approximately 500 individuals were arrested for drug trafficking—175 of them were confirmed members of the Gulf Cartel. Agents also seized $60.1 million in U.S. currency, 36,841 pounds (16,711 kg) of cocaine, 1,039 pounds (471 kg) of methamphetamine, 19 pounds (8.6 kg) of heroin, 51,258 pounds (23,250 kg) of marijuana, 176 vehicles, and 167 weapons.

According to Michael B. Mukasey, U.S. Attorney General under President George W. Bush, "Although I am pleased with the efforts so far, we cannot and will not rest on these successes. The threat posed by international drug cartels is too great. It will take all of us working together to prevail."[2]

Despite the success of Project Reckoning, authorities say the cartel remains strong. The Gulf Cartel is

Drug Trade in the Media

The drug trade is often the focus of movies, television, and books. *Bad Boys II, Maria Full of Grace, Traffic, Blow, Miami Vice,* and *American Gangster* are some films that feature drug trafficking. The television series *The Wire,* which began airing in 2002, depicts aspects of the drug trade in Baltimore, Maryland. Books that depict drug use and the drug trade include the young adult novel *Go Ask Alice* and the crime thriller *The Power of the Dog.*

well established around the world. If drugs cannot be sent along one trade route, they can easily be sent by another path.

The DEA makes arrests and seizures frequently. It confiscates millions of dollars and thousands of pounds of drugs. In 2007, the agency carried out at least nine major operations.

Even so, the drug trade continues to thrive. When one group is taken down, another usually takes its place. Many people wonder if anything can be done to prevent the spread of the drug trade and the continued violence associated with it.

Items seized in a 2004 drug bust in Chicago, Illinois, included heroin, marijuana, weapons, and money.

A person rolling a marijuana joint, or cigarette

ILLEGAL DRUGS

Despite efforts to curb drug use in the United States, the country remains the largest consumer of illicit, or illegal, drugs. According to the National Survey on Drug Use and Health, nearly 20 million U.S. residents over the age of 12 are drug users. Some of the most popular drugs include marijuana, cocaine, heroin, methamphetamines, LSD, and Ecstasy.

MARIJUANA

Marijuana is a product of the hemp plant, *Cannabis sativa* or *Cannabis indica*. The plant contains approximately 400 chemicals. The main chemical in marijuana is tetrahydrocannabinol, or THC.

Most often, marijuana users smoke the leaves and buds of the hemp plant in cigarettes or pipes. The leaves can also be mixed into food or tea. Smoking marijuana produces a faster effect than eating it does. However, the drug's effect may last longer when it is eaten. Hashish is another product of the hemp plant. This sticky resin of the plant is a more concentrated form of the drug. Like marijuana, hashish can be smoked or eaten.

Use, Abuse, Dependence, Addiction

Although drug use, abuse, dependence, and addiction are often used interchangeably in non-technical contexts, each word has a specific definition. Drug use applies to any situation in which a drug is taken. Drug abuse happens when the nonmedical use of a drug interferes with the user's life. Dependence is a more general term that describes situations in which the user must take the drug to function. Addicts are dependent on their drugs. Drug addiction means that the user cannot stop taking the drug. Addiction can be physical, if the body needs the drug. This type of addiction can cause physical withdrawal symptoms if drug use stops. Addiction can also be mental. These addicts will crave the drug but will not necessarily experience physical withdrawal symptoms.

After smoking marijuana, the heart's rate can increase by 20 to 50 beats per minute. After the THC enters the brain, the user may feel a sense of euphoria or experience pleasant sensations. Colors and sounds may seem more intense. Other effects can include thirst, hunger, cold, or trembling hands. After the euphoria passes, the user may feel tired or depressed. For some people, the effects of marijuana use do not feel pleasant. Instead, these users may experience anxiety, fear, panic, or paranoia.

Some studies have shown that, over time, marijuana can cause a user to become dependent on the drug. It can impair a person's ability to learn and pay attention. Because marijuana is most often smoked, it can cause lung problems in chronic users.

Cocaine

One of the more addictive drugs is cocaine. This powerful drug is

Steroids and Performance-Enhancing Drugs

Anabolic steroids are sometimes prescribed to cancer and AIDS patients to aid cellular growth. However, because they also help promote muscle development, they can be used as performance-enhancing drugs for athletes. Most major sports organizations ban the use of anabolic steroids by their athletes because it gives them an unfair advantage. In the United States, anabolic steroids are illegal without a prescription.

Other performance-enhancing drugs can help build muscle mass. Human growth hormone is one example. Certain stimulants, painkillers, and diuretics may also be considered performance enhancing. It is usually up to individual athletic organizations to define which drugs—and how much of those drugs—give athletes an unfair advantage.

Powerfully addictive cocaine is a white powder that users often snort through the nose.

extracted from the coca plant. The white powder can be snorted through the nose or dissolved in water and injected. Crack is cocaine that has been processed to a freebase, or more pure, form. The crack rock crystals can be smoked.

Cocaine's effects are immediate. The drug creates a euphoric feeling and increases energy and mental clarity. When injected or smoked, the drug reaches the brain quicker than when snorted. This may cause the effects to be more intense, but they will last for a shorter period. Cocaine users may experience tremors, muscle twitches, paranoia, or dizziness. They may exhibit erratic or violent behavior—particularly if the user goes on a binge without sleep for extended periods. After the drug leaves the brain, users often "crash," or feel irritable and depressed.

Long-term use of cocaine can create a strong feeling of paranoia. Users are also at risk of death by cardiac or respiratory arrest. Cocaine addicts can become depressed and have intense cravings for the drug. It is often very difficult for them to stop using cocaine.

HEROIN

Heroin is in a class of drugs called opiates. These drugs, which are often prescribed as painkillers, can be extremely addictive. The most popular drug among all of the opiates, heroin is a powerful depressant, which means it makes the user feel relaxed. Heroin is processed from morphine, a chemical found in poppy plants. Heroin is usually injected into a vein or a muscle. It can also be smoked, inhaled, or snorted. The effects of the drug are felt within a few seconds of injection. The user will feel euphoria, a warm flush, and heaviness.

Often, heroin is cut, or mixed, with other less expensive substances. Heroin may be cut with sugar or powdered milk. It may also be cut with poisons, such as strychnine or fentanyl. Mixing heroin with substances that appear similar increases the amount of product dealers can sell. This increases their profits. It also makes the drug less potent. Also, because heroin users do not know how much of the drug they are taking, they are often at risk of overdosing.

Chronic heroin users can develop heart disease. They may also have complications from the unknown substances used to cut the heroin. Users often share their needles, which increases their risk of contracting hepatitis, HIV/AIDS, and other diseases. After a user stops taking the drug, he or she may experience intense withdrawal symptoms that can last a week.

METHAMPHETAMINE

Some drugs, such as methamphetamine, are produced in labs or cooked in dangerous makeshift kitchens. Methamphetamine, often

Opiates

Drugs containing opium are part of a class of drugs called opiates. Opium comes from the poppy plant and was used as early as 5000 BCE. It has been used as a recreational drug and a pain reliever in all parts of the world, from China to Europe to the Middle East. It has been a source of great conflict in these regions.

Today, opium is used to make medical drugs such as morphine and codeine. Opium and its derivatives are popular recreational drugs in many parts of the world.

simply called meth, is most often made from pseudoephedrine, a common decongestant found in cold and allergy medication. Meth comes in white or yellow rocklike chunks. The powder that flakes off the rocks can be eaten, injected, snorted, or smoked.

Meth increases heart rate and alertness and decreases appetite. Meth stimulates the release of large amounts of dopamine in the brain. Dopamine is a chemical that stimulates brain cells and creates a good feeling. Meth damages the brain's ability to produce this feel-good chemical. In the long-term, this can result in depression and other mood disorders. Chronic meth users may also show symptoms of violent behavior, hallucinations, insomnia, and paranoia.

LSD

LSD is a common hallucinogenic drug. It is made from lysergic acid, which can be found in certain types of fungus. The drug is taken orally and sold as tablets, a liquid, or on absorbent paper.

Hallucinogenic drugs such as LSD can alter perception, mood, and personality. The effects are often unpredictable. While some users may feel euphoria, others may react with terror and panic.

The user may see things that are not there, causing them to act strangely or dangerously. Users also report unusual sensations, such as "hearing" colors and "seeing" sounds. Other effects may include increased body temperature and heart rate, dilated pupils, sweating, and loss of appetite.

LSD is not known to be addictive, but a user may soon need larger quantities of the drug to experience the same effects. Heavy users may have an increased risk of developing depression or schizophrenia. Users also report having flashbacks

Prescription Drug Abuse

Legal drugs also run the risk of being abused. In many cases, a patient may be prescribed painkillers, tranquilizers, or other drugs to fight an illness. However, some of these drugs have abuse potential and properties that can lead to dependence or physical addiction.

Amphetamines, analgesics (pain relievers), barbiturates, and tranquilizers are prescription drugs that may be abused. Opiate-based pain relievers such as OxyContin, Percocet, and Vicodin are the most commonly abused prescription drugs.

This type of drug abuse is becoming more common. The National Institute on Drug Abuse reports that approximately 48 million people ages 12 and older have taken prescription drugs for nonmedical reasons. That is approximately 20 percent of the U.S. population. In 2007 alone, 5.2 million people used pain relievers for nonmedical purposes. Experts are unsure of the reason for the increase in prescription drug abuse. However, they point to ease of access as a likely contributor. Online pharmacies make obtaining these drugs without a prescription easier. Some people are under the false impression that if a doctor can prescribe it, the drug must be safe—even if it is misused.

Alcohol and tobacco are the most commonly abused drugs, though adults may purchase them legally. Alcohol is a depressant. It also impairs judgment and coordination. People who abuse alcohol may become dependent on it. Alcoholics have physical symptoms of withdrawal when they are not drinking. Alcoholism is a chronic disease that often requires counseling or other treatments.

Tobacco is a legal drug that is addictive. Tobacco contains nicotine, a stimulant. Nicotine addiction causes withdrawal symptoms in users. Smoking damages the lungs, the heart, and the blood vessels. Chronic smokers may develop respiratory problems or lung cancer. Tobacco kills more people in the United States each year than all other legal or illegal drugs combined.

of their experiences using the drug. These flashbacks may occur years later, even after drug use has stopped.

Ecstasy

Ecstasy is one of the most popular among a group of drugs known as club drugs or designer drugs. Ecstasy is classified as a stimulant, but it can also cause hallucinations. The drug comes in tablet form and is taken orally.

As its name suggests, Ecstasy can make the user feel intense pleasure, peacefulness, and exhilaration. Ecstasy is often used at parties, raves, and clubs to give the user energy to dance all night. Other effects include jaw clenching, dehydration, blurred vision, chills, or impaired judgment. Ecstasy use can be fatal when it leads to heart failure, seizures, or acute dehydration. Aftereffects of Ecstasy use can include depression, anxiety, sleep problems, or paranoia.

A sheriff showing some of the hazardous household chemicals used
to produce methamphetamine

A user injecting drugs with a needle

ADDICTION AND SOCIETY

espite the negative side effects of illegal drug use, users seek the euphoria it can bring. However, the euphoria does not last long. Drug users may become abusers or addicts, and many struggle to quit.

What Is Addiction?

Some people become physically dependent on a drug. Without it, they feel sick and have trouble functioning or living normally. Other people become mentally dependent on a drug. The drug takes an important role in their lives. They develop strong cravings for the drug and will seek it out despite the consequences.

Not all drug users are abusers. A person might try a drug once or twice and never use it again. Not all drug abusers are addicts. Drug abusers do not make healthy choices regarding drug use, but they are not necessarily dependent on the drug. To varying degrees, genetics, the environment, and the person's mental state play a role in whether a drug abuser will become addicted. But any person who abuses drugs is in danger of experiencing negative side effects of drug use or becoming addicted.

**Dependence
and Popular Drugs**

A 1994 study ranked some of the most commonly used drugs in order of the likelihood that users would become dependent on them. Nicotine was rated the highest, followed by heroin, cocaine, alcohol, and caffeine.

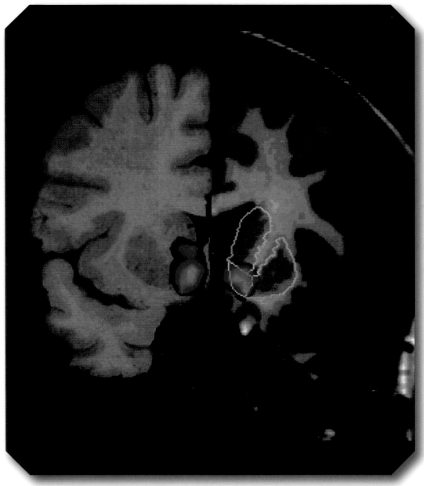

A brain scan shows the effects of cocaine on the brain. The thin yellow line shows the brain circuits stimulated by the drug.

Drugs that cause addiction affect the brain. They flood the person's brain with dopamine. This chemical is normally released when a person is experiencing something pleasurable, such as playing with a pet or eating a candy bar. Drugs can create a similar, and often greater, feeling of pleasure. According to Clare Stamford, an expert in the biology of addiction,

> *People continue to take drugs because they like what the drugs do and want to keep on taking more. Unfortunately, people keep taking drugs because if they don't, they get plummeted into a withdrawal syndrome which can be uncomfortable and life threatening.* [1]

After continued use, the brain gets used to having the drug in its system. Chemicals that would naturally release dopamine fail to do so. The brain has become dependent on the drug, and the drug user has become addicted.

ADDICTS AND SOCIETY

Drugs take a central role in an addict's life. Addicts will spend a great deal of time and money to

Drugs and Newborns

Pregnant women who use drugs risk passing their addictions on to their unborn children. In 2005, an estimated 4 percent of pregnant women used illicit drugs during their pregnancy. Depending on the extent of the drug use, infants might go through withdrawal after birth. Some do not survive.

Any exposure to drugs puts a child's health at risk. Infants exposed to drugs during development may have a low birth weight, deformities or congenital defects, or stunted physical and mental development.

Getting Help

Addicts do not usually recognize they have a problem. Many times, it is up to loved ones to confront users about their behavior. If a drug abuser or addict is arrested in connection with his or her drug use, the user may be forced by the courts to get treatment. Some people may need to go through detoxification, or be medically supervised while they go through withdrawal. In some cases, medication can help an addict stop using dangerous drugs. Addicts also need therapy or counseling to help them through their addictions. Many addicts will relapse, or return to their drug use. Support groups, such as Alcoholics Anonymous and Narcotics Anonymous, can help addicts stay away from drugs.

obtain and use drugs. They might choose drugs over their family, friends, and jobs. Women who use drugs while pregnant put their unborn children at risk. Drug users may become violent and harm themselves and others while using drugs. Many cases of child abuse and spousal abuse are related to drugs.

Crime surrounds drug use on all sides. Many people go to jail for using or selling drugs. In addition, many addicts will turn to crime to pay for their drug habits. Theft, prostitution, and drug dealing are crimes often associated with drug abuse. Gangs and other drug trafficking organizations fight over territory and profits, causing increased violence. This criminal activity puts a strain on police as well as the justice system. In 2004, 17 percent of inmates in state prisons were serving time for drug-related crimes. Courtrooms and prisons are crowded with criminals who have been arrested for drug-related crimes.

Drug abuse also puts a burden on the health care system. Drug users may contract or spread disease by sharing used needles. Often, they cannot afford to pay for their health care. They may rely on government assistance programs, or they may not pay the bill if hospitalized.

A History of Drugs

Although drug abuse is an issue in today's society, drug use is not a new phenomenon. Human beings have used drugs for thousands of years. Records of poppy, or opium, in ancient Babylonia date back to 5000 BCE. Hashish was widely used in Persia during the eleventh century. In Western China, marijuana has been used in rituals for 2,700 years. For hundreds of years before Europeans made their way across the Atlantic

Pure Food and Drug Act

No drugs were illegal in the United States until the twentieth century. The first federal law regarding drug use was the Pure Food and Drug Act of 1906. The act required that products be labeled with their ingredients. Prescription and nonprescription drugs now had to list the amounts of opiates, cocaine, marijuana, and other substances they contained. The act did not, however, prohibit the use of such drugs. The federal government began making certain drugs illegal in the 1910s, beginning with opium and cocaine.

Ocean, Native Americans grew tobacco and chewed or smoked it regularly.

By the nineteenth century, the drug trade had become a global business. Rum was a major export of the Caribbean islands, and tobacco was being sold to Europe as the United States' main crop. Britain sold huge amounts of opium to China in the late eighteenth and early nineteenth centuries even though the drug was prohibited by Chinese law.

At the same time, cocaine

The Opium Wars

One of the first efforts to control the drug trade occurred in China during the nineteenth century. The British East India Company held a profitable monopoly on opium trade from India to China. The Chinese rulers tried to end the monopoly. They felt that opium use was immoral and incited greed and crime. They worried the British would try to use the trade to control them in other ways. When the monopoly was finally broken, however, opium trade actually increased. Merchants from France and the United States were eager to compete with the British in this market. Low-priced opium was widely available on the streets of China.

Chinese rulers decided to stop the opium trade completely. But when they demanded that foreign merchants hand over their supplies of this drug, the British objected. The First Opium War, also known as the First Anglo-Chinese War (1839–1842), broke out. China lost and was forced into several treaties with Britain, France, and the United States. Several small battles, known as the Second Opium War, happened from 1856 to 1860. The Treaty of Tientsin was signed in 1858, forcing China to accept imported opium. The treaty also established a tariff on imported opium that gave the Chinese government a share of the profits. To avoid the tariffs, an illegal opium trade developed. Smuggling gangs became powerful secret societies in China.

and opium were making their way into the world of medicine. They were hailed as cure-alls, and their addictive qualities were mostly ignored. Morphine was used liberally among American Civil War doctors to relieve wounded soldiers' pain. Unfortunately, almost 400,000 soldiers became addicted to the substance. In this time, there were no laws prohibiting drug use in the United States. All drugs were legal and easily available. By the twentieth century, many countries faced problems with drug abuse.

As some countries began limiting the drug trade, illegal smuggling spread. In 1909, U.S. President Theodore Roosevelt met with representatives from 13 nations in Shanghai, China, to discuss the illegal drug trade. This meeting resulted in an agreement between the countries at the Hague Convention in 1913 and 1914 to regulate the worldwide opium trade.

Snake Oil

Until the early twentieth century, salesmen roamed the country hawking potions and pills promising miraculous cures. Called snake oil or patent medicine, these remedies usually had no real medical benefits. Liquids, lotions, or lozenges, the quack remedies consisted of oil, wax, or lard, plus various blends of herbs and spices. Most drinkable varieties contained large proportions of alcohol, and some contained cocaine or opiates. The alcohol and other drugs made people feel better, though these ingredients could not really cure any illnesses. Snake oil grew less popular in the United States after the 1906 Pure Food and Drug Act required the salesmen to label the ingredients on their bottles and the public learned what actually went into their cure-alls.

After World War I, the responsibility of regulating the drug trade was given to the League of Nations. The United Nations and the World Health Organization took over in 1946. But as laws were passed at both national and international levels, the drug trade went increasingly underground. It was becoming more difficult to control.

Drug users gathered in opium dens in San Francisco, California, in the 1880s.

A Peruvian farmer watched his coca crop dry in the sun. In some parts of the world, plants used to produce drugs are the most profitable crops.

DRUG PRODUCTION

Today, drug trafficking remains a difficult problem to control. In part, this is because the drug trade is a global enterprise. The majority of drugs used in the United States are grown and produced in foreign nations.

The United States does not have the authority to enforce drug laws in other countries. However, it can use economic pressure to make countries cooperate by refusing to trade with them or give them aid. The United States must work with international organizations and local governments to get to the source of the problem.

However, in some countries, drug production is the most profitable industry. If production were reduced, the economy of those countries would be in trouble. Poor farmers must have a better way to feed their families if they are to stop growing crops for drugs.

SOUTH AMERICA

Colombia, Peru, and Bolivia are the leading producers of cocaine. The coca crop grows well in the soil of the Andes Mountains, though it also thrives in more tropical environments. It can be harvested

Traditional Coca Use

The indigenous people of the Andes have grown coca for thousands of years. They chew the plant's leaves or use the leaves to make tea. The plant is mildly stimulating. Unprocessed coca leaves do not have nearly the same effects as processed cocaine and are much less dangerous. Today, some farmers in Bolivia are still legally allowed to grow coca for traditional purposes.

regularly, ensuring a steady income for the peasants who farm it.

South American governments try to reduce the supply of coca by providing farmers with alternative crops to plant instead. The government also destroys coca crops by uprooting them or spraying them with herbicide, or weed killer. The military may even shoot down planes carrying coca to be processed into drugs at refining plants.

Celestino Quispe is a coca grower in Bolivia. Quispe has considered growing coffee or citrus fruits instead of coca, but he says those crops would not bring in enough money to support his family of five:

> *Coca is a means of survival for us. Because the soil is very tired, very eroded. Coca leaves are the only option we have for earning a living to feed ourselves and our families.*[1]

In addition, coca is easy to transport and sell, and a small amount is worth a lot of money. In rural areas with poor roads and difficult access to markets, it is much harder to transport and sell the large amounts of fruits or vegetables needed to equal coca's profits.

Most coca farms in Colombia are located in the southern portion of the country. They are protected by soldiers from guerrilla military groups involved in the drug trade. Cocaine is a $6 billion industry in Colombia. An estimated 90 percent of the cocaine that enters the United States is grown there. Because so much coca is being grown in the country, efforts to reduce the supply have little impact. Despite herbicide spraying from airplanes, there is at least as much coca being grown in Colombia as when these efforts started. In fact, the drug trade in the country is expanding. In recent years, Colombia has

Alternative Crops

One way to fight drug production is to promote alternative crop development. If farmers harvested food crops rather than opium or coca, they would reduce the supply of the raw material for drugs.

The United Nations Office on Drugs and Crime (UNODC) estimates that approximately 3 million people rely on illicit crops for their income. Typically, these people live in poverty. Opium and coca crops bring in more money than food crops would. They do not think they can risk switching to an unproven crop and still feed their families. If a new crop is introduced, it must match the needs and the skills of the people in the area. The crop must also be able to thrive in the harsh climates farmers sometimes face. Rural areas must have roads and markets for farmers to transport and sell their crops.

Although illicit crops provide farmers with a good source of income, the UNODC argues that they do not create a sustainable living. The income gained from the crops may not help much in times of food shortages. Farmers also have to pay a share of their profits to drug traffickers and guerrilla groups. By growing illicit crops, farmers are often breaking the law. They risk having their crops destroyed or, worse, receiving jail time.

become a leading supplier of opium as well.

THE GOLDEN TRIANGLE AND THE GOLDEN CRESCENT

The world's opium supply comes chiefly from two areas known as the Golden Triangle and the Golden Crescent. The Golden Triangle consists of the Southeast Asian countries of Burma, Laos, and Thailand. Afghanistan, Iran, and Pakistan make up the Golden Crescent.

In the Golden Triangle, Burma was the leader in opium supply for a long time. Afghanistan, in the Golden Crescent, became a strong competitor in 2002 after severe drought damaged Burma's poppy crops. Burma's opium production has also been reduced by government actions, such as sending groups of soldiers to destroy poppy fields. However, the government faces many

Drugs in the Golden Triangle

Efforts to control opium production in the Golden Triangle seem to be successful in some ways. Although some years see a rise in opium production, in recent years production has mostly fallen. Economic pressure from other nations and a crackdown on farmers helped decrease production. A switch to amphetamine production by drug lords in the Golden Triangle may have had the greatest impact on the decline of the opium industry. In 2009, however, the United Nations Office on Drugs and Crime (UNODC) warned that unless the region's economy improved, opium production would rise again.

A farm laborer in Afghanistan cut poppy heads in order to collect their resin. Poppies are used to produce opium.

challenges. It does not have the funds necessary to supply its military to match the well-funded drug lords. Also, opium is produced in remote areas of the country that are not easily reached.

Burma's efforts seem to be working, or perhaps the drug trade has merely shifted to other countries. In the 1970s, the Golden Triangle produced up to 70 percent of the world's opium. By 2007, the area produced only 5 percent of the world's supply. The Golden Crescent has taken over as the leading supplier of opium.

In 2008, Afghanistan was the world's leading opium supplier. The poppy plant from which opium is made requires little water, making it a good crop for Afghanistan's arid climate. The country produced more than 6,724 tons (6,100 t) of opium in 2006, and production has generally continued to increase. Although the drug trade is banned in the country, the Afghan economy relies on it. Also troubling is that profits from drug production often fund terrorist activities.

Drug use in Afghanistan was illegal under the Taliban, a fundamentalist group that ruled Afghanistan from 1996 to 2001. Use of heroin, hashish, or alcohol could result in a prison sentence. Smoking tobacco was strongly discouraged. Despite the Taliban's moral opposition to drug use in its own country, however, it encouraged continued drug production. Taliban leaders argued that it was up to other nations to prevent illegal drug use within their own borders.

In 2001, the Taliban was ousted from power. After several years of rule by a transitional government, Hamid Karzai became the country's president in 2004. Under the new government, opium production was illegal. However, the new government has not been successful controlling production.

Morocco

Morocco is one of the leading producers of cannabis, the crop used to make marijuana and hashish. The plant grows well in Morocco's soil and climate. But the Moroccan government is making efforts to decrease production. Local farmers could face jail time for growing cannabis. Many continue to harvest the profitable crop in order to feed their families.

Abdeslam Dahmane works with the United Nations Office on Drugs and Crime (UNODC).

Drugs and Terrorism

The Taliban government was in control of Afghanistan from 1996 to 2001. The Taliban supported al-Qaeda, the group responsible for the terrorist attacks of September 11, 2001. The Taliban was removed from power in 2001, but terrorist groups continue to receive much of their funding from the sale of opium. This is especially troubling to the United States. When drug users purchase opium products, such as heroin, they may provide the Taliban with financial support.

According to Dahmane, "There have been lots of past attempts to find alternative crops, but they haven't always worked, because cannabis is a crop that commands such an inflated price."[2]

Despite these difficulties, production has declined dramatically, possibly because of the severe government crackdowns. In 2007, the UNODC reported a 50 percent decrease in production of cannabis in Morocco. However, demand remains high. It remains to be seen if the Moroccan government will be able to continue the production decrease, or if this progress is only temporary.

THE NETHERLANDS

Amsterdam is often referred to as the drug capital of the world because of its loose drug laws. Marijuana is legal in the country and can be purchased in small amounts for personal use. Despite looser drug

The UNODC Crop Monitoring

The UNODC works with the governments of drug-growing countries, including Peru, Colombia, Bolivia, Burma, Laos, Afghanistan, and Morocco. Together, they monitor illicit crops. They track the size and location of the crops. This helps the countries determine the best strategy for combating the production of drug crops.

laws, the Netherlands has a lower rate of marijuana use than the United States has.

The Netherlands is also a leading producer of synthetic drugs, such as Ecstasy and amphetamines. Most of the Ecstasy in Europe comes from the Netherlands, and imports to the United States are increasing. Synthetic drugs are gaining popularity in Europe and North America, especially among young people.

The Dutch government makes a distinction between soft drugs, such as marijuana, and hard drugs, such as Ecstasy and heroin. Soft drugs are technically illegal, but the laws against them are not enforced. However, the Dutch government enforces tough laws against hard drugs. Preventing the production of synthetic drugs is challenging, as they do not depend on a single crop. Rather, several ingredients are needed to produce

Drug Tourism

The Netherlands is known for its relaxed marijuana policies and cannabis coffee shops, where marijuana is sold openly to customers. The country has become a tourist destination for those who want to smoke marijuana without fear of prosecution. In 2008, the Dutch border cities Bergen op Zoom and Roosendaal announced plans to close their coffee shops to reduce drug tourism, which is believed to increase drug-related crime.

the drug. In addition, locating labs is difficult because they move often. Trafficking routes also change frequently. ⌐

Marijuana plants growing in a greenhouse inside a home
in Tijuana, Mexico

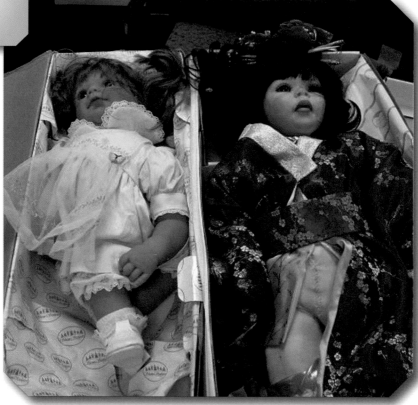

Smugglers hide drugs in unlikely places, such as inside these dolls, which were used to hide methamphetamine.

TRANSPORTING DRUGS

The constant flow of drugs across borders is difficult to police. U.S. borders are deserted in many areas. Because the drug trade is very profitable in the United States, it attracts many ruthless and sophisticated drug traffickers.

How Drugs Are Smuggled

After drug crops are harvested, they are sold to drug traffickers. Drugs may cross borders as raw materials or as processed drugs. Sometimes, drug smugglers can cross borders in isolated areas where they will not meet border security, guards who search travelers' bags for drugs and other illegal materials. In most cases, drugs must be moved along ordinary roads and trade routes. Smugglers find ways to pass through security without being found.

Large quantities of drugs are often shipped in cargo containers that seem to hold legal cargo. It is not possible for inspectors to examine every container that crosses U.S. borders. If guards do not check the containers, the drugs can pass easily into the country. Other times, the drugs are concealed in these containers. The drugs may be hidden inside a shipment of toys or buried under a shipment of coffee or produce. If the cargo is inspected, it may look innocent, and the scent of the drugs may be masked by other odors.

Drug Tunnels

Tunnels crossing under the border into the United States from both Mexico and Canada are used for drug smuggling. They also serve as passages for illegal immigrants to enter the United States. These tunnels are long and narrow. In some cases, they are reinforced with wood supports and even have lighting. The passages provide relatively safe travel for drug traffickers and immigrants. Since the 1990s, law enforcement agencies have discovered more than 30 such tunnels.

Drug organizations often hire people not directly involved with the cartel to carry drugs across borders. They are often known as mules. They may hide the drugs in their belongings or on themselves. The organizations lure these mules with the promise of thousands of dollars. However, this payment is only a fraction of the value of the drugs they are carrying. A drug mule can carry hundreds of thousands of dollars worth of drugs.

According to Porota, a Colombian woman who worked as a drug mule, the cartels train the smugglers to swallow balloons filled with drugs. Porota was caught smuggling drugs into England and was sent to prison. When asked about her work as a drug mule, she said:

Dangers of Smuggling

In addition to risking jail sentences, drug mules risk their health. These smugglers swallow large quantities of drugs wrapped in rubber or latex balloons. If one of the balloons breaks inside a mule's body, he or she is exposed to an extraordinary amount of drugs. Drug mules exposed to drugs in this way have died of an overdose before medical help could arrive. For drug trafficking organizations, the drugs inside the mule's body are more important than the person's safety. Mules have been discovered near airports with their stomachs ripped open and emptied of the drugs.

Drug smugglers are also in danger of violence by the drug organizations for which they work. Smugglers may be tempted to keep the drugs and sell them at a higher price. If the drugs are lost or the smuggler refuses to continue to work for the organization, they or their families might face retaliation.

I carried drugs because I had no help supporting my children and things were very difficult for us. You will do whatever you have to do for your children. I wanted them to have a better life, without so much hardship.[1]

POLITICAL INSTABILITY

Drug trafficking routes often go through countries that are poor, politically unstable, or both. Such nations do not have the resources to investigate or defend against drug-related crimes. Also, stopping drug trafficking is not usually a priority for governments that are fighting wars.

Drug organizations are often more powerful and better funded than the governments that resist them. Government officials can be easily paid off to allow illegal activity. Another problem is that the heavily armed guerrilla groups involved in drug trafficking contribute to political instability if they become stronger than their country's government.

Haiti

Sometimes, Colombia's cocaine also travels to the United States through Haiti. The government of Haiti is politically unstable and therefore weak. This makes the country a good area for Colombian drug organizations to traffic their drugs. Cocaine can reach U.S. tourists in the Caribbean through this important port. The drug may also be transported by ship to Miami, Florida.

This woman worked as a drug mule until she was caught and sent to prison.

THE SOUTHERN U.S. BORDER

The large amounts of cocaine produced in South America most often come into the United States through Mexico. Drug cartels are not afraid to use violence to protect their illegal business, and the U.S.-Mexico border is an especially violent area as cartels war with government troops and with each other. The Mexican government is facing a considerable increase in violent crime, including muggings, firefights, kidnappings, murders, and assassinations. Although much of the violence occurs on the Mexico side of the border, U.S. officials consider the increased violence a threat to national security and the safety of U.S. citizens.

Mexico's president, Felipe Calderón, has made controlling the drug cartels a priority since he took office in 2006. He has also requested more money from the U.S. government to pay for troops to protect the border. Calderón works closely with Colombia's president, Álvaro Uribe, who has arrested more than 900 individuals and sent them to the United States for trial. Colombia is the primary source of the cocaine that flows through Mexico and into the United States.

Other Major Hubs

China is a major hub for the Asian drug trade. Poppies grown in Burma are transported to drug labs on the border of Thailand and China, in territory controlled by militant Chinese drug organizations. The heroin produced in these labs is then taken across borders by way of the Mekong River. However, drug organizations also transport

Canada

The U.S.-Canada border is also an entry point for illicit drugs. The two nations work closely to combat drug use, production, and distribution. Like the United States, Canada is a big consumer of illicit drugs. Canada is also a producer of high-potency marijuana and synthetic drugs.

heroin via the Pacific Ocean. And drug mules travel through Rangoon International Airport in Burma to distribute heroin to the global market.

Afghanistan is a landlocked country, which means drugs produced there must go over land routes. Much of the heroin produced in Afghanistan goes through Iran and the Balkans before it reaches the European market. The border is poorly guarded, making it easy for mules to slip through. If traffickers do run into problems, they will also use machine guns and grenades to force their way past border security.

International Day against Drug Abuse and Illicit Trafficking

The UNODC celebrates International Day against Drug Abuse and Illicit Trafficking on June 26. The day is a way to raise international awareness of the problems associated with drug use and drug trafficking. Each year's campaign has a different focus. In 2007, it was drug abuse. Drug cultivation and production were the focus in 2008, and drug trafficking was the topic in 2009.

After the drugs pass through Iran, they go through Turkey and the Balkan nations, including Romania, Serbia, and Macedonia. The governments of these nations are unstable due to war during the 1990s. They cannot fight the Turkish drug organizations that control the drug trade in this region. These organizations also provide labs with the chemicals to refine drugs.

Mexican president Felipe Calderón worked to stop drug trafficking in his country.

Federal agents raided a house in California where they believed members of a Mexican drug cartel lived.

DRUG TRAFFICKING ORGANIZATIONS

*D*rug trafficking organizations control the profits from drugs. Often, they use their money and firearms to overpower local governments. These organizations are important to maintaining the drug trade and its continued success.

What Are Drug Syndicates?

Drug syndicates are also called drug trafficking organizations, drug cartels, and drug gangs. They can vary in both scope of influence and size. Some drug syndicates are specialized. Their influence may be limited to one area of drug trade, such as production or controlling local law enforcement. Other drug syndicates control the entire operation from start to finish. Some large organizations may rival an entire nation's government in size and funding. Because many drug syndicates operate in countries that are politically unstable or weak, drug syndicates may be more powerful than the government.

The largest drug syndicates can purchase illicit crops directly from the farmers who grow them. The syndicates sell drugs to dealers in the United States and Europe. As law enforcement increases, trafficking drugs becomes riskier. As the risk increases, traffickers charge more money for their products. As the price of drugs increases, more people want to profit from drugs. Drug trafficking becomes more profitable, and the cartels become larger and more powerful.

Essential Issues

INFLUENCE

Depending on their location, drug syndicates sometimes operate with relative freedom. In South America, for example, many governments do not have the money or law enforcement agents to patrol their huge areas of jungle, mountains, and wilderness. Drug traffickers run drugs down the Amazon River from Colombia with little resistance. They also use small planes that are difficult to detect.

In other cases, drug cartels may be able to pay off high-ranking government officials and law enforcement agents to ignore their illegal activities. These organizations can also afford high-priced lawyers to defend their top businessmen. In this way, drug syndicates can exercise some control over even those governments that are working against the cartels.

"By spreading dangerous drugs and resorting to brutal violence, international drug cartels pose an extraordinary threat both here and abroad."[1]
—Former U.S. Attorney General Michael B. Mukasey

VIOLENCE

Drug syndicates can also exercise their control through violence, such as that in Mexico. More than 10,000 people died in Mexico because of drug-related violence between December 2006 and June 2009. Government officials and reporters who publicly oppose the drug syndicates may receive death threats against themselves and their families. Violence between rival gangs or between gangs and police forces spills into the

Colombian Drug Cartels

Because Colombia provided most of the cocaine smuggled into the United States, cartels in the country were very powerful from the 1970s through the 1990s. The Medellín and the Cali were two of the most dangerous cartels in South America during this period.

The Medellín cartel smuggled large quantities of cocaine to the United States in small airplanes. Huge profits allowed the cartel to develop sophisticated labs and better airplanes. The Cali cartel was the Medellín's main rival. The Cali operated quietly, running successful legal businesses to cloak their illegal activities.

Colombian police and the U.S. Drug Enforcement Administration (DEA) brought down the two cartels in the 1990s. They tracked down and arrested many of the cartels' leaders.

Hundreds of small, difficult-to-catch organizations have since emerged. The Revolutionary Armed Forces of Colombia (FARC) is a revolutionary guerrilla organization. It uses profits from cocaine to fund some of its operations. The organization is known for violence and kidnappings of Colombian citizens. The United Self-Defense Units of Colombia (AUC) is made up of independent paramilitary groups, many paid for by drug lords. Its members are heavily involved in the drug trade and responsible for many killings. FARC and AUC are at war with each other and the Colombian government.

In 2000, the U.S. government helped make the biggest jungle drug bust in Venezuela at the time.

streets, sometimes injuring bystanders. There are few people willing to stand up to the drug trade in an atmosphere of fear.

Drug syndicates are often well armed because they use the same methods for smuggling drugs to participate in the illegal firearms trade. In many cases, drug syndicates have both access to firearms and an eagerness to use violence.

Money Laundering

Because of the illicit nature of their business, drug trafficking organizations must conceal the sources of their income. Law enforcement agencies often track money to discover how a drug syndicate works. The trail of money from one bank account to the next can lead law enforcement to drug lords.

Money laundering is an important part of any drug trafficking organization. It involves concealing the true source of income through methods such as fake businesses, real estate purchases, and bank deposits. If the income appears to be legally obtained, it is less likely that law enforcement will be able to trace it to the drug trade.

In some cases, businesses may think that they are participating in legitimate transactions. However, they may actually be enabling a

Fear in Mexico

According to a 2008 poll by the BBC World Service, 42 percent of Mexicans felt less safe than they did the previous year. The influence of drug cartels, crime, and social inequality were issues that concerned many Mexican citizens. Despite the efforts of the Mexican government, drug-related violence has increased in Mexico since 2007. When one cartel is taken down, others fight to take its place, leading to greater violence. Thirty-seven percent of those polled said they had considered leaving Mexico because of the drug cartels.

criminal organization to launder money. Money laundering weakens the economy and enables corruption. It is another component of drug trafficking that hurts society.

Museum of Drugs

The Museum of Drugs opened in Mexico City in 1985. The museum shows the various roles drugs play in the lives of Mexican citizens. Exhibits includes actual drugs, notes from peasant farmers asking soldiers not to destroy their illicit crops, and examples of ways drugs are smuggled into the United States. The displays show that the drug problem in Mexico is complex and influences the lives of millions of people. The museum is run by the military and is not open to the public.

THE ARELLANO-FELIX FAMILY

Although drug trafficking organizations operate in all areas of the world, the Drug Enforcement Administration (DEA) recognizes those in Mexico as the biggest threat to the United States. These organizations dominate the drug trade in every area of the country, except the northeast. But they are gaining greater influence there.

The Arellano-Felix Organization, also known as the Tijuana cartel, is one of the most dangerous drug syndicates in Mexico. The organization smuggles cocaine, heroin, marijuana, and methamphetamines across the border into California.

The organization fell into the hands of seven brothers and four sisters after the arrest of the former leader, Miguel Angel Felix Gallardo, in 1989. After that, the Arellano-Felix Organization gained a reputation for its extreme violence— including torture, execution, and kidnapping. The cartel may have employed police officers who conducted surveillance on behalf of the cartel and carried out some of its kidnappings.

Ramon Arellano was the organization's most visible leader during the late 1990s and early 2000s. In 2002, Arellano was shot and killed by police. Other members of the family were captured and arrested. The last brother was arrested in 2008. Officials believe the Arellano-Felix Organization has been weakened by the loss of its leaders. Now, the organization has split into two groups that are fighting

Money Laundering Online

The Internet has made money laundering more difficult to track. Payment can be made through Web-enabled cell phones anonymously. Online role-playing games that use fake digital currency offer another way for payments to be made without tracking an individual's true identity. Digital currency can be exchanged for real money from the game company.

for control. This has allowed rival cartels in Tijuana to expand their own operations. These rival cartels are more difficult to stop than the Arellano-Felix organization was. ⌐

SEEKING INFORMATION

On the Drug Trafficking and Money Laundering related activities of the Aréllano-Félix Organization

Fernando
Sánchez-Arellano

Armando
Villarreal Heredia

Manuel Invanovich
Zambrano-Flores

ARELLANO-FÉLIX HOTLINE

Toll-Free from USA

1-800-720-7775

Collect/Direct from Mexico

001-858-277-4215

All calls answered by U.S. Agents
All calls confidential

Email: afotips@usdoj.gov

Issac Manuel
Godoy-Castro

Melvin
Gutierrez-Quiroz

Raymundo
Corona-Bartolome

Fernando
Avila-Valenzuela

Eduardo Teodoro
Garcia-Simental

Reydel
López-Uriarte

José Filiberto
Parra-Ramos

This poster asks for information about ten people identified
as drug traffickers.

Police arrested suspected gang members in New Jersey in 2008.

DRUG DEALERS
AND USERS

Once illegal drugs reach the United States, local gangs or other criminal organizations take possession of the drugs. These groups are responsible for selling the drugs to individual users.

Drugs on U.S. Streets

Violent street gangs and outlaw motorcycle gangs are heavily involved in dealing illicit drugs on U.S. streets. Most gangs sell drugs in their neighborhoods, but a few sell on a national level. Two of these so-called supergangs, the Bloods and the Crips, operate in more than 100 U.S. cities. And because profits from selling illicit drugs are often better in smaller cities, these gangs continue to spread into residential neighborhoods.

Because the drug trade is so lucrative, many street gangs focus their activities around it. They are highly organized and resemble traditional businesses to some extent. Only top members are able to acquire substantial wealth. Many individuals join gangs as poorly paid street-level dealers, hoping that one day they will be able to move up within the organization.

Outlaw Motorcycle Gangs

Motorcycle clubs first emerged after World War II. They began as social groups whose members were interested in motorcycles. However, many of these groups grew violent and became involved in illegal activities. Four of these clubs have been designated as outlaw motorcycle gangs by the Federal Bureau of Investigation: the Hells Angels, the Outlaws, the Bandidos, and the Pagans Outlaw. These groups are heavily involved in drug trafficking, including drug dealing and manufacturing methamphetamine.

Street gang activity can lead to violence when one gang trespasses on another's turf. Gangs typically sell drugs in designated areas, but they are always trying to expand their territory to increase profits. During turf wars, gunfire may erupt on open streets. Smaller attacks between rival gang members can go on for weeks. This sort of activity endangers the community and can discourage local businesses.

DRUG-RELATED CRIME

Turf wars are not the only drug-related crimes. Of course, possessing, using, and selling drugs are all illegal, but drug use is

What Is a Gang?

A gang is a group of people who participate in organized criminal activity. Many gangs form in low-income or inner-city neighborhoods. People may join because they want to belong to a community. Street gangs are typically identified by a common name, color, sign, or symbol.

Gangs may participate in stealing, vandalizing property, drinking alcohol, and using drugs. Some gangs participate in drug trafficking. These gangs are often more likely to fight over territory and kill rivals.

A gang may start out as a loosely structured group and become more organized as it participates in more complex criminal activity. Gangs that deal illicit drugs are often very structured. They may have a president, a vice president, and a treasurer in the top positions. These members are often paid very well. However, they are also targets for law enforcement and lower members looking to advance within the organization. Low-ranking, or street-level, gang members may deal drugs directly to users or watch for the police. These gang members are often paid very poorly—less than minimum wage. They are also in the most dangerous positions, working openly on the street and fighting in turf wars.

closely linked to other criminal activities.

Drug-induced crimes are motivated by the user's desperate need to obtain drugs at any cost. For example, drug users may steal money to buy drugs. Also, some drugs may cause users to become violent or paranoid; they may attack other people or destroy property.

According to the U.S. Department of Health and Human Services, people are more likely to commit crimes when they are using drugs. A study by the department found that individuals who used drugs in the past year were 16 times more likely to be arrested for larceny, or theft, than nonusers. They were also nine times more likely to be arrested for assault.

Drug Users

In 2007, the National Survey on Drug Use and Health reported

Youth PROMISE Act

In 2007, Congressman Robert Scott of Virginia introduced the Youth PROMISE Act. The act would provide money for communities to create programs to keep children and teens out of gangs and out of jail In 2009, the act was still under consideration by Congress.

The Federal Bureau of Investigation (FBI) considers Hell's Angels an outlaw motorcycle gang because of its criminal activities.

that 19.9 million U.S. residents age 12 and older had used an illicit drug in the past month. This represents 8 percent of the U.S. population. More than 112 million of those surveyed reported having used an illicit drug at least once.

The study found that marijuana was the most commonly used illicit drug, with 14.4 million users in the past month. It was followed by psychotherapeutics (such as pain relievers or tranquilizers) with 6.9 million users; cocaine with 2.1 million users; hallucinogens (including Ecstasy) with 1 million users; inhalants (including paint and household cleaners) with 600,000 users; and heroin with 200,000 users in the past month.

Drug use varies according to a person's age, race, and social group. These characteristics influence the likelihood that an individual will use drugs and the types of drugs he or she may use. For example, cocaine is an expensive drug popular with upper-class drug users. Crack is an inexpensive form of cocaine, making it more attractive to low-income drug users.

Young adults are the most likely group to use drugs. In 2007, approximately 20 percent of adults ages 18 to 25 were illicit drug users.

Addiction Stories

People who have battled addiction often share their stories to discourage others from abusing drugs. Jennifer Romano began using meth when she was 18 years old. Her addiction ultimately destroyed her marriage and her relationships with her children, friends, and family. Romano recalls, "[My husband and I] were moving in and out of houses, staying with our parents and relatives, and using drugs the entire time. We left our children behind because we were so hooked; we thought of nothing else but ourselves and our next fix."[1]

Out of almost 20 million drug users in the United States, 14.4 million of them use marijuana.

The majority of them were employed either full-time or part-time. Of the 17.4 million drug users age 18 or older, 13.1 million (75 percent) were employed.

In terms of race, drug use is the biggest problem among American Indians, with 12.6 percent of persons age 12 and older using illicit drugs.

In comparison, 11.8 percent of people reporting two or more races, 9.5 percent of African Americans, 8.2 percent of whites, and 6.6 percent of Hispanics or Latinos report using drugs in the past month. Asians report the lowest rate of drug use, at 4.2 percent. The high percentage of American Indians reporting drug use can be attributed at least in part to the historic poverty on reservations.

These general usage statistics do not necessarily match levels of prosecution or incarceration for drugs. Despite their similar usage statistics, African Americans are prosecuted and jailed for drug offenses at a much higher rate than whites are for the same crimes.

EFFECTS OF DRUG USE

The drug trade thrives because drug users continue to demand drugs and are willing to pay high prices

The 1960s

Drug use increased dramatically in the 1960s in the United States. Society was undergoing great turmoil and changes, including the civil rights movement and the Vietnam War. Many teens and young adults rebelled against traditional society. For many of these people, the rebellion included recreational drug use, especially LSD and marijuana.

for them. For many, using drugs is a social activity. People use drugs to belong to a group and have fun. Others use drugs as an escape. For them, drug use provides a temporary break from their problems.

By purchasing illegal drugs, users allow dangerous drug cartels and street gangs to operate and threaten the lives of innocent people. But most drug users do not consider the consequences of supporting this illegal trade.

Users also may not consider personal risks, such as becoming dependent or addicted. Addiction can destroy personal relationships as well as a person's health. Illegal drugs can also cause unexpected side effects. Users may not tell their doctors about having taken drugs. Doctors may not be able to treat them effectively without this information. ⌒

OVER SEVEN YEARS FOR SELLING CRYSTAL METH.

WAS IT WORTH IT?

IT'S YOUR LIFE; DON'T THROW IT AWAY.
DON'T BREAK THE LAW.

WILLIAM CULLUM

A poster created by the U.S. Attorney's Office warns of the possible consequences of selling methamphetamine.

President Nixon speaking with members of the National Advisory Council for Drug Abuse Prevention

THE WAR ON DRUGS

he U.S. government has been fighting drug use in the United States since the early twentieth century. Consumption of alcohol was illegal from 1920 to 1933, during the era known as Prohibition. During the 1960s, the United

States saw a dramatic increase in recreational drug use and street crime. Colombian drug cartels were also coming into power. U.S. President Richard Nixon identified drug use and drug trafficking as serious threats to the United States. In 1971, Nixon first declared that the country was in a war on drugs.

THE DRUG ENFORCEMENT ADMINISTRATION

The Drug Enforcement Administration (DEA) was established in 1973 as part of U.S. efforts to fight the war on drugs. Nixon described the need for such an organization:

> *Right now, the federal government is fighting the war on drug abuse under a distinct handicap, for its efforts are those of a loosely confederated alliance facing a resourceful, elusive, worldwide enemy. Certainly, the cold-blooded underworld networks that funnel narcotics*

Changing Drug Laws

Although President Jimmy Carter (1977–1981) had considered legalizing marijuana, during the 1980s, President Ronald Reagan (1981–1989) took a hard-line stance against drug use. At the time, marijuana was considered a "gateway" drug. In other words, marijuana use would lead to harder drugs, such as heroin. If marijuana use was treated as a serious criminal offense, it was believed that fewer people would do it. Ideally, this would prevent them from moving on to more dangerous drugs. In response, some states passed laws against owning or selling drug paraphernalia, or equipment, such as water pipes, syringes, and papers for rolling cigarettes. Since Reagan's time in office, many experts have come to believe that the gateway theory is not accurate.

from suppliers all over the world are no respecters of the bureaucratic dividing lines that now complicate our anti-drug efforts.[1]

"Imagine a world without drugs. . . . Our mission at the DEA is to do every-thing possible to make that world a reality. We do it with strong enforce-ment—cutting off the drug supply at its source—working with our local law enforcement partners here . . . [and by teaching] citizens just how sinister [bad] the drug culture has become and how drugs terrorize neighborhoods and destroy lives. How a youthful 'experimenta-tion' too often becomes a deadly addiction."[2]

—Michele Leonhart,
acting administrator of
the DEA, October 2008

The agency is responsible for handling all aspects of the drug problem, from drug addiction to drug trafficking. The DEA uses agents from other government agencies, including the U.S. Customs Agency and the Central Intelligence Agency (CIA).

The DEA investigates the drug trade, both in the United States and abroad. Different parts of the DEA focus on exposing separate aspects of the drug trade. The DEA also works with drug enforcement organizations in other countries. Sometimes, DEA agents work undercover. They pose as members of the drug cartels they want to bring down. As they become trusted members, these agents can acquire information on cartel leaders and large drug deals.

PREVENTION

Some organizations focus on preventing people from using drugs in the first place. During the 1980s, First Lady Nancy Reagan launched her well-known "Just Say No" campaign. Since then, drug education and drug awareness programs have made their way into the majority of U.S. public schools. The U.S. government has even sponsored national televised advertising campaigns against drug use. These kinds of programs raise awareness about the drug problem. However,

D.A.R.E.

Drug Abuse Resistance Education (D.A.R.E.) was founded in 1983 to educate schoolchildren about the consequences of drug abuse. As part of the program, police officers talk to students about resisting peer pressure to use drugs. The D.A.R.E. program is used in 75 percent of U.S. schools. Millions of students have participated in the program.

D.A.R.E. is one of the best-known drug prevention programs. By educating students about drugs at a young age, parents and teachers hope to influence students against using drugs when they get older. Students are informed about the various types of drugs and their negative side effects. And they are warned about the dangers of addiction. The program also teaches students to resist peer pressure.

Despite the program's popularity, skeptics wonder if D.A.R.E. has any real effect on an individual's future drug use. Though drug use has declined since D.A.R.E.'s inception, drug education is also more widely available. Researchers at the University of Kentucky studied graduates of D.A.R.E. ten years after completing the program. They concluded that D.A.R.E. has no greater effect than drug education during regular health classes.

Nancy Reagan, center, meets with people in New Hampshire to promote her drug prevention program in 1987.

their effectiveness at preventing future drug use is questionable.

Another measure some schools take to prevent drug use is random student drug testing. In these schools, students who wish to participate in sports or other extracurricular activities are required to take the random tests. Some school administrators say that such testing can prevent students from using drugs because students know there is a good chance they will be caught. Other experts have found that random drug testing might actually increase teen drug use. Afraid they will face drug tests, some teens may simply avoid after-school activities. Teens without structured activities after school are more likely to use drugs or be involved in other risky behaviors.

Harsh punishments for drug users are another way to discourage drug use. If people know they could face jail time for simply possessing illegal drugs, they may be less likely to use drugs.

In addition, some drug addicts are ordered to go through rehabilitation, or therapy, to quit using. Simple detoxification can help rid the drugs from an addict's system. The next step may be to address what drives the patient to use drugs in the first place. Additional treatment to manage other problems in an addict's life may prevent him or her from turning to drugs again. Some addicts have mental issues that encourage their drug use, while others need job training or education to help them function in normal society. But helping addicts is well worthwhile for many reasons. One of them is to reduce the demand for illegal drugs in the United States.

"We must stand with our families to help them raise healthy, responsible children. And when it comes to helping children make right choices, there is work for all of us to do. One of the worst decisions our children can make is to gamble their lives and futures on drugs."[3]
—*George W. Bush*
State of the Union
Address
January 20, 2004

A student undergoes random drug testing in Great Britain.

AN INTERNATIONAL EFFORT

While prevention focuses on reducing the
demand for drugs, most law enforcement efforts
focus on reducing the supply of drugs. Because
drug trafficking is a global problem, U.S. law
enforcement agencies must work in cooperation
with other nations to solve it. The United Nations
Office on Drugs and Crime (UNODC) helps
organize nations so that they can work together to
combat the drug problem as best they can. Many of
the countries where drug trafficking takes place have

weak governments, however. They do not have the resources to combat the powerful drug cartels.

In 2008, the U.S. designated $400 million to aid Mexico in combating the drug problem. However, because the drug industry brings in more than $6 billion annually, even this aid may not be enough.

Has the War on Drugs Failed?

The war on drugs is costly. Public money goes to multiple areas, including the law enforcement agencies that investigate the drug trade and the judiciary system that prosecutes offenders. Taxpayer dollars also fund the prisons that house criminals and the hospitals that care for unhealthy drug users. Some treatment facilities for addicts also receive public money. All told, some estimates put the cost of the war on drugs as high as $75 billion per year.

According to Michele Leonhart, the acting administrator of the DEA in 2009, the agency has had a positive impact on the drug trade. Leonhart explains:

> *DEA has proven that we can—and are—destroying powerful drug organizations. . . . We have seized record amounts of*

drugs, cash, and assets, which has had tremendous impact—from fewer drugs on the street, to millions of dollars kept out of the hands of criminals and terrorists, to fewer dangerous drugs in the hands of our children, and less violence in our communities. [4]

However, others do not believe the costly war on drugs is effective. Harsher enforcement drives up the risk for drug cartels. In response, drug prices rise, making the trade more profitable and encouraging more people to get involved. Other critics say that people will always seek out and use drugs.

DEA Museum

The DEA operates a museum in Arlington, Virginia, outside Washington DC. The museum was established as part of a government effort to educate U.S. residents about the work of various government agencies. The museum's first exhibit, "Illegal Drugs in America: A Modern History," opened to the public in 1999. The DEA hopes to show museum visitors the complex and devastating role drug use has played in U.S. history.

As an example, they point to the unsuccessful period of Prohibition in the United States, when alcohol consumption was outlawed. According to Ethan A. Nadelmann, director of the Drug Policy Alliance, a drug-policy research institute, "The 'war on drugs' has failed to accomplish its stated objectives, and it cannot succeed so long as we remain a free society, bound by our Constitution." [5]

*Despite large drug busts, not everyone agrees that the war
on drugs is working.*

Protestors called for federal legalization of medical marijuana
in Los Angeles, California, in 2007.

REFORMING THE
DRUG LAWS

The war on drugs is an ongoing battle with no end in sight. The U.S. government has taken a tough stance, spending billions of dollars combating the drug problem. Even so, millions of citizens continue to use drugs, and the drug trade continues to thrive. If the United States is going to win the war on drugs, changes to current drug policies may be necessary.

LEGALIZATION

For some, the answer to the U.S. drug problem is a simple one: make drugs legal. If the drug trade were a legal business, they argue, it would be regulated and easier to monitor, similar to the way tobacco and alcohol are sold. Drug users would know their drugs were not cut with dangerous poisons. They would also be able to tell their doctors about their drug use without fear of punishment.

One philosophy of drug control is known as "harm reduction." This philosophy assumes drugs will not disappear from society, so the best practice is to minimize the harm drugs cause. Harm-reduction programs could include comprehensive treatment for addicts who seek it, clean needle exchanges, and new methods in drug-prevention education. Doctors and public health officials would take a more active role in combating the drug issue by helping manage addiction and drug use.

Because drug use is an individual's choice, many people see the prohibition of drugs as a violation of civil liberties. Such prominent individuals as Milton Friedman, Hugh Downs, and Archbishop Desmond Tutu have endorsed this viewpoint. They say that, in most cases, drug use does not cause significant harm to the user or to others. Drug users should be allowed to make their own decisions about their lifestyles.

Some people argue drugs should be decriminalized. Although drugs would remain illegal, users would not be prosecuted unless they committed additional crimes. Decriminalization supporters recognize that

---

Needle Exchange Programs

The first needle exchange programs were established during the late 1980s as part of an effort to combat AIDS. Needles used to inject drugs are responsible for the transmission of approximately one-fifth of all HIV infections and most hepatitis C infections. In some places, syringes are considered drug paraphernalia. Individuals may not possess syringes without a medical prescription.

Needle exchange programs allow people to dispose of used syringes and obtain new sterile syringes at no cost and without fear of arrest for illegal drug use. The programs also provide such services as HIV/AIDS education, testing for HIV and other infectious diseases, condom distribution, drug rehabilitation referrals, and other social services.

Reports have found that needle exchange programs effectively prevent the spread of infectious diseases such as HIV/AIDS, and they do not contribute to drug use. In most cases, individuals who want to inject themselves with drugs would do so with or without sterile needles. Despite these findings, the U.S. Congress has banned federal funding of needle exchange programs since 1988. This ban has made it difficult for such programs to continue to operate.

drug use can be very harmful.
However, they feel many people are
punished more severely than they
should be under the current drug
laws. In October 2008, Mexican
President Felipe Calderón proposed
decriminalizing small-time drug use.
John Walters, director of the White
House Office of National Drug
Control Policy (ONDCP), supported
this proposal.

Under the George W. Bush
administration (2001–2009),
drug laws were enforced severely.
President Barack Obama has

"Our prohibitionist approach to drug control is responsible for most of the ills commonly associated with America's 'drug problem.' And some measure of legal availability and regulation is essential if we are to reduce significantly the negative consequences of both drug use and our drug-control policies."[1]
—*Ethan A. Nadelmann,
director of the Drug
Policy Alliance*

considered relaxing drug sentencing in certain cases.
And with the Mexican government considering
decriminalization policies, the war on drugs may
change to address these new approaches to drug use.

The Netherlands, Belgium, Portugal,
Luxembourg, Italy, and Spain have changed their
laws to decriminalize marijuana. Users in these
countries might face such penalties as having their
driver's licenses revoked or paying hefty fines, but
they are not sentenced to jail time.

Vermont Attorney Robert Sand speaks to the American Civil Liberties Union about decriminalizing drug use.

Many experts look at the drug trade in these countries to predict what effect federal decriminalization would have on the United States. In European countries with decriminalization

policies, marijuana use is similar to those with strict
regulations against the drug.

MEDICAL MARIJUANA

One drug that some people would like to see
legalized is marijuana. The National Organization
to Reform Marijuana Laws (NORML) supports the
legalization of marijuana. NORML and other groups
that advocate legalized marijuana argue that the drug
is less harmful than legal drugs such as tobacco and
alcohol. Marijuana is also far less addictive than
tobacco or alcohol. By legalizing marijuana, law
enforcement could focus on dealing with hard-drug
users, they argue.

In addition, marijuana provides some benefits
in treating illnesses. Marijuana can provide relief
to patients with AIDS, cancer, multiple sclerosis,
glaucoma, and depression. In 1996, California
became the first state to legalize the medical use of
marijuana. As of 2008, 13 U.S. states had approved
the use of medical marijuana.

Still, marijuana remains an illegal substance
under federal law, and the Food and Drug
Administration has not approved it for medical
purposes. Federal law enforcement agents have been

known to raid dispensaries of medical marijuana, arresting the owners and seizing the drugs.

U.S. President Barack Obama has pledged to end the federal government's raids on clinics that dispense medical marijuana in states that have approved the practice. A spokesman for Obama told reporters,

> *Obama supports the rights of states and local governments to make this choice— though he believes medical marijuana should be subject to [U.S. Food and Drug Administration] regulation like other drugs.*"[2]

Beginning in March 2009, the U.S. attorney general announced that the Justice Department would stop raiding medical marijuana clubs.

ARGUMENTS AGAINST LEGALIZATION

With any drug, some lawmakers fear that legalization could lead to increased use. Legalization could

Environmental Impact

The drug trade can also have a devastating effect on the environment. Drug enforcement agencies often spray illicit crops with herbicides that also destroy food crops. In addition, herbicides seep into the soil and can contaminate the water supply. This can cause problems in the eco-system and with public health.

According to the government of Colombia, in order to produce one gram (.04 oz) of cocaine, 4.8 square yards (4 m²) of rain forest have to be cleared. Since 1988, 5.44 million acres (2.2 million ha) of Colombian forest have been cut down to grow coca.

make some people think that the drugs are not dangerous. They say that teenagers would have greater access to drugs, just as they are able to acquire cigarettes and alcohol when they are underage. According to ONDCP Director John Walters:

> *Some people believe drugs such as cocaine and heroin should be legal, sold by the government and regulated like alcohol. Our experience with alcohol (some 127 million regular drinkers as compared to fewer than 20 million drug users) suggests this would be a huge mistake. It is hard to imagine an aspect of American life that would be enriched by millions of new cocaine, heroin or marijuana users.[3]*

An Ongoing Issue

Drugs have pervaded society for centuries. It is unlikely that any policy could completely end drug use. But because of its harmful effects on society and public health, lawmakers hope to limit it.

New Jim Crow?

African Americans make up about 12 percent of the U.S. population. However, 38 percent of drug arrests and 59 percent of drug convictions involve African Americans. Because the drug policies seem to target African Americans unfairly, some critics call U.S. drug policies the new Jim Crow laws. Jim Crow laws mandated racial segregation in some parts of the United States between 1876 and 1965.

The drug trade is a global operation that is highly lucrative. When one drug cartel is taken down by law enforcement, another is always ready to take its place. This makes it difficult for governments to make a significant impact on the drug trade. As long as people continue to use them, drugs will be trafficked for tremendous profits. The problem has no end in sight. Many wonder how to best curb the drug trade while still protecting the safety and rights of individuals.

While most agree that illicit drugs pose problems for society, few agree on the best way to solve these problems.

TIMELINE

5000 BCE	1800s	1839
First written accounts document opium use.	The British East India Company monopolizes the opium trade from India to China.	The First Opium War begins.

1910s	1913–1914	1920–1933
The U.S. government passes laws to make drugs illegal, beginning with opium and cocaine.	Worldwide regulation of opium trade is ratified at the Hague Convention.	Alcohol use is prohibited in the United States.

1858	1861–1865	1906
The Treaty of Tientsin is signed, legalizing the importation of opium to China.	About 400,000 American Civil War soldiers become addicted to morphine.	The Pure Food and Drugs Act becomes the first federal law regarding drug use in the United States.

1946	1960s	1971
The United Nations and the World Health Organization become regulators of the international drug trade.	Drug use and street crime in the United States increase dramatically.	President Richard Nixon declares that the United States is in a war on drugs.

TIMELINE

1973	1977–1981	1980s
The Drug Enforcement Administration is created.	President Jimmy Carter considers decriminalizing marijuana use.	The first needle exchange programs are established to help fight the spread of diseases such as HIV/AIDS.

1996	1999	2001–2009
California voters approve the use of medical marijuana.	The Drug Enforcement Administration Museum opens to the public.	President George W. Bush enforces harsh laws against drugs.

1981–1989

President Ronald Reagan takes a firm stand against drugs

1983

Drug Abuse Resistance Education (D.A.R.E.) is founded to educate schoolchildren about the consequences of drug abuse.

1993

Pablo Escobar of the Medellin cartel is killed by police. Terrorist organization FARC takes over some of the Medellin territory.

2002

Ramon Arellano is killed by police. Rival cartels expand into former Arellano-Felix organization territory.

2004

In the United States, 17 percent of inmates at state prisons are serving time for drug-related crime.

2008

The United States grants $400 million to Mexico to fight drug trafficking.

ESSENTIAL FACTS

AT ISSUE

❖ The U.S. war on drugs costs billions of dollars each year, but the drug trade remains very active.

❖ The drug trade is deeply rooted in the global economy.

❖ The drug trade encompasses many different aspects. Law enforcement must combat the drug trade by going after farmers, producers, smugglers, drug trade organizations, dealers, and users.

❖ Drug trafficking organizations are often very powerful and extremely dangerous. They often operate in countries with weak governments, and they are often able to corrupt local law enforcement.

❖ Decriminalization or legalization of drug use might be an effective way to control drug trafficking because it would make the drug trade easier to monitor. However, softening the laws may make drug use seem more socially acceptable and lead to increased drug use.

CRITICAL DATES

1700–1800s
The international trading of drugs became important to countries' economies.

Early 1900s
The United States and other countries began regulating drug use.

1940s
The United Nations and the World Health Organization were given the responsibility of regulating international drug trade.

1971
U.S. President Richard Nixon officially declared the United States to be in a war against drugs. Since the 1970s, some presidents have enforced drug laws more harshly than others.

1973
The U.S. Drug Enforcement Administration (DEA) was created. The DEA uses agents from other government agencies, including the Bureau of Narcotics and Dangerous Drugs, the U.S. Customs Agency, the Central Intelligence Agency, and the Office of Drug Abuse Law Enforcement.

1970s–1980s
The Medellín cartel rose to power in Colombia. The cartel was known for being violent. Similar cartels operate all over the world.

1996
Medical marijuana use was approved by California voters. As of 2008, 13 states had approved the medical use of marijuana. However, the drug remains illegal under federal law.

Quotes

"DEA has proven that we can—and are—destroying powerful drug organizations. . . . We have seized record amounts of drugs, cash, and assets, which has had tremendous impact—from fewer drugs on the street, to millions of dollars kept out of the hands of criminals and terrorists, to fewer dangerous drugs in the hands of our children, and less violence in our communities."—*Michele Leonhart, acting administrator of the DEA*

"The 'war on drugs' has failed to accomplish its stated objectives, and it cannot succeed so long as we remain a free society, bound by our Constitution."—*Ethan A. Nadelmann, director of the Drug Policy Alliance*

ADDITIONAL RESOURCES

SELECT BIBLIOGRAPHY

Baum, Dan. *Smoke and Mirrors: The War on Drugs and the Politics of Failure*. Boston: Little Brown, 1996.

Drug Policy Alliance Network. 2008. 24 Feb. 2009 <http://www.drugpolicy.org/>.

"Frontline: Drug Wars," *NPR*. 2001. <http://www.pbs.org/wgbh/pages/frontline/shows/drugs/>.

"The Global Drugs Trade," *BBC News*. 2008. <http://news.bbc.co.uk/hi/english/static/in_depth/world/2000/drugs_trade/default.stm>.

Gray, Mike. *Drug Crazy: How We Got Into This Mess and How We Can Get Out*. New York: Random, 1998.

Meyer, Kathryn, and Terry Parssinen. *Webs of Smoke: Smugglers, Warlords, Spies, and the History of the International Drug Trade*. New York: Rowman and Littlefield, 1998.

Siegel, Ronald K. *Intoxication: The Universal Drive for Mind–Altering Substances*. New York: Park Street, 2005.

FURTHER READING

Bauder, Julia. *Drug Trafficking*. Detroit: Greenhaven. 2007.

Dudley, William. *The History of Drugs: Marijuana*. Detroit: Greenhaven. 2004.

Landau, Elaine. *Meth: America's Drug Epidemic*. New York: Twenty-First Century. 2007.

Web Links

To learn more about drug trafficking, visit ABDO Publishing Company online at **www.abdopublishing.com.** Web sites about drug trafficking are featured on our Book Links page. These links are routinely monitored and updated to provide the most current information available.

For More Information

For more information on this subject, contact or visit the following organizations.

Drug Enforcement Administration
800 K Street NW, Suite 500, Washington, DC 20001
202 305 8500
www.usdoj.gov/dea/index.htm
The Drug Enforcement Administration enforces U.S.-controlled substance laws. The organization provides information about drug trafficking, drug policy, and drug use prevention.

Drug Policy Alliance
70 West 36th Street, 16th Floor, New York, NY 10018
212-613-8020
www.drugpolicy.org
This organization is working to end the war on drugs by minimizing the harm caused by drug use.

Partnership for a Drug-Free America
405 Lexington Avenue, Suite 1601, New York, NY 10174
212-922-1560
www.drugfree.org
This organization provides information and resources to prevent drug use.

Glossary

abuse
Nonmedical drug use that interferes with the user's life.

addiction
Drug use that the user cannot stop, for physical or mental reasons.

black market
The buying and selling of illegal goods or services.

cartel
An association of manufacturers or suppliers who work to limit competition and keep prices high.

decriminalize
To remove the criminal penalties against something.

dependence
Needing a drug to function.

depressant
A drug that slows the body's processes.

detoxification
A medical treatment during which a patient receives counseling and abstains from drug use until he or she is no longer physically dependent on the drug.

drug-related crime
A crime that is motivated by a user's need to use drugs or by the drug's effects.

economy
The financial system of a country, a region, or an area.

hallucinogen
A drug that causes hallucinations or confuses the senses.

illicit
Illegal or not allowed.

legalization
To make legal or lawful.

money laundering
Concealing the source of money obtained illegally.

monopoly
Exclusive control of a market.

mule
A person paid to carry drugs illegally into a country.

narcotic
An addictive drug that reduces pain, causes sleep, or changes mood and behavior.

opiate
A drug that contains opium or other chemicals that are made from opium.

Prohibition
The period (1920–1933) during which alcoholic beverages were outlawed in the United States.

raw material
An unprocessed natural product used in manufacturing.

smuggle
To transport goods secretly.

stimulant
A drug that quickens the body's processes.

tariff
A tax on imported goods.

traffic
To trade or deal a certain commodity, which is often illegal.

tranquilizer
A drug that can relax a person without putting them to sleep.

withdrawal
Symptoms associated with quitting drugs, such as headache, diarrhea, and tremors.

SOURCE NOTES

Chapter 1. The Drug Trade
1. "Interview Bill Alden." *Frontline: Drug Wars.* 2008. WGBH
Educational Foundation. 30 Oct. 2008 <http://www.pbs.org/
wgbh/pages/frontline/shows/drugs/interviews/alden.html>.
2. "175 Alleged Gulf Cartel members Arrested in Massive
International Law Enforcement Operation." *U.S. Drug Enforcement
Administration Web site.* 17 Sept. 2008. U.S. Drug Enforcement
Administration. 30 Oct. 2008 <http://www.usdoj.gov/dea/pubs/
pressrel/pr091708.html>.

Chapter 2. Illegal Drugs
None.

Chapter 3. Addiction and Society
1. Richard Hollingham. "The Nature of Addiction." *BBC News
World Edition.* 2003. 20 Nov. 2008 <http://news.bbc.co.uk/2/hi/
health/784033.stm>.

Chapter 4. Drug Production
1. "My Story: The Coca Grower." *BBC News.* 6 June 2000. 20 Nov.
2008 <http://news.bbc.co.uk/2/hi/americas/779662.stm>.

2. Richard Hamilton. "Morocco's War on Cannabis." *BBC News.*
9 Mar. 2007. 20 Nov. 2008 <http://news.bbc.co.uk/2/hi/
africa/6426799.stm>.

Chapter 5. Transporting Drugs
1. "My Story: The Drug Smuggler." *BBC News*. 8 June 2000. 26 Nov. 2008 <http://news.bbc.co.uk/2/hi/779728.stm>.

Chapter 6. Drug Trafficking Organizations
1. "175 Alleged Gulf Cartel Members Arrested in Massive International Law Enforcement Operation." *U.S. Drug Enforcement Administration Web site*. 17 Sept. 2008. U.S. Drug Enforcement Administration. 30 Oct. 2008 <http://www.usdoj.gov/dea/pubs/pressrel/pr091708.html>.

Chapter 7. Drug Dealers and Users
1. Jennifer Romano. "Demon of Choice." *Partnership for a Drug-Free America*. 24 Aug. 2005. 1 Dec. 2008 <http://www.drugfree.org/Portal/DrugIssue/MethResources/demon_of_choice.html>.

Source Notes Continued

Chapter 8. The War on Drugs

1. "1970–1975: Creation of the DEA (July 1, 1973)." *U.S. Drug Enforcement Administration Web site*. U.S. Drug Enforcement Administration. 2 Dec. 2008 <http://www.usdoj.gov/dea/pubs/history/1970-1975.html>.

2. "Target America: Opening Eyes to the Damage Drugs Cause." *U.S. Drug Enforcement Administration Web site*. 1 Oct. 2008. U.S. Drug Enforcement Administration. 2 Dec. 2008 <http://www.usdoj .gov/dea/speeches/s100208.html>.

3. "George W. Bush on Drugs." *On the Issues.* 27 Feb. 2008. 7 Dec. 2008 <http://www.ontheissues.org/Celeb/George_W_Bush_Drugs .htm>.

4. Michele M. Leonhart. "Acting Administrator's Message." *U.S. Drug Enforcement Administration Web site*. U.S. Drug Enforcement Administration. 2 Dec. 2008 <http://www.usdoj.gov/dea/speeches/ aa_message.pdf>.

5. Ethan A. Nadelmann. "The War on Drugs Is Lost." *National Review.* 12 Feb. 1996. 2 Dec. 2008 <http://www.nationalreview .com/12feb96/drug.html>.

Chapter 9. Reforming the Drug Laws

1. Ethan A. Nadelmann. "The War on Drugs Is Lost." *National Review.* 12 Feb. 1996. 6 Dec. 2008 <http://www.nationalreview .com/12feb96/drug.html>.

2. Bob Egelko. "Next President Might Be Gentler on Pot Clubs." *San Francisco Chronicle.* 12 May 2008. 8 Dec. 2008 <http://www.sfgate.com/cgi-bin/article.cgi?f=/c/a/2008/05/12/ MNKK10FD53.DTL>.

3. John Walters. "Our Drug Policy Is a Success." *Wall Street Journal.* 5 Dec. 2008. 8 Dec. 2008 <http://online.wsj.com/article/ SB122843725720181453.html>.

INDEX

Index Continued

ABOUT THE AUTHOR

Jill Sherman is the author of several books for young people. She has a BA in English from the College of New Jersey. Jill lives and works in Toms River, New Jersey.

PHOTO CREDITS

Martin Mejia/AP Images, cover; Elaine Thompson/AP Images, 6; Mike Calamung/AP Images, 11; AP Images, 12, 28, 48, 65, 75, 95; M. Spencer Green/AP Images, 15; Matthew Fearn/PA Wire/AP Images, 16; Steve Parsons/PA Wire/AP Images, 19, 96; Sue Ogrocki/AP Images, 25; Paul Faith/PA Wire/AP Images, 26; North Wind Picture Archives/Photolibrary, 35, 96; Martin Mejia/AP Images, 36; Murray Brewster/AP Images, 41; Guillermo Arias/AP Images, 47; William Fernando Martinez/AP Images, 52; Eduardo Verdugo/AP Images, 55; Cuauhtemoc Beltran/AP Images, 56; Andres Leighton/AP Images, 60; Mel Evans/AP Images, 66, 99; Robert Galbraith/Reuters/Corbis, 70; Mike Stewart/AP Images, 72, 98; Henry Burroughs/AP Images, 76, 97; Jim Cole/AP Images, 80, 99; Sang Tan/AP Images, 82; Ric Feld/AP Images, 85; Richard Vogel/AP Images, 86; Toby Talbot/AP Images, 90